Forest Bonsai

Craig L. Hunter
VenatorScribe

Copyright © Craig L. Hunter, 2017.   All rights reserved
ISBN 978-0-473-35202-8

CONTENTS

Preface	4
The Genesis of a Bonsai	7
From saplings to trees	9
Suitable selection	11
Constructing a bonsai forest	12
Pot, slab or slab-pot selection	13
Tie-down systems & drainage control	14
Foliage Pruning	15
Various pruning techniques	17
Reducing leaf size and promoting trunk forks	18
The five plant hormones controlling size	21
Defoliate with care	24
Wiring	25
Root pruning and planting the forest	29
Root Pruning and Planting the Forest	30
Meteorological seasons	32
Positioning in the pot	33
Techniques borrowed from the art world	38
Transplant shock	39
Willow water	42

Muck and Moss	44
Water - Drainage - Soil	49
Signs of overwatering and dehydration	50
Drainage	51
Root rot	53
Happy holidays	54
Insects and Biodiversity	55
Pantry based fungicide	56
Chewing insects	57
Leaf piercing and sucking insects	57
Leaf rasping and sucking insects	58
Biodiversity	60
Two step treatment approach	62
As Winter Descends	63
Rapid and extreme temperature changes	66
Low temperature injury - 'frost crack'	66
Conifers - winter burn sun scald	67
Natures Setting	68
How to Diagnose a Bonsai Obsession	70
Copyright and fine print	71

Preface

The general aesthetics we expect to see in every bonsai, seem insufficient when we think in terms of a bonsai forest. When it comes to creating a standard bonsai, we want the tree to project a scene that captivates the observer with it's aura of elegance and simplicity. However with a bonsai forest we should attempt to reflect an element of nobility, reflecting the majestic looking forests we find in nature. A bonsai forest might not replicate the individuality of both style and character that is typical of a potted bonsai, however it is no less challenging to create. With a forest planting, there are additional factors to consider, such as density of planting, balance, depth, perspective and focal point. These visual design elements provide a fresh range of exciting new dimensions and challenges to the art of bonsai. This alone makes it worthy of our skills to have at least two or more bonsai forests in amongst your collection of trees. The central concept for this book is the use of three and four year old saplings to create a number of bonsai forests. Additionally there is also the option of using young plants from commercial nurseries such as dwarf junipers and azaleas. These trees, in their infancy, can be acquired at low prices. However you need to be selective and only use trees with good trunk characteristics. For example, an interesting bonsai forest can be created using flowering trees such as azaleas, to replicate the flowering Rhododendron forests of the Himalayas. A forest of Persian Silk trees, will similarly provide a dense and delicate canopy of pink flowers. Equally a very small and effective forest can be created using dwarf Conifers after de-neddling the trunks. And if you don't have enough saplings to create a one specie forest there is the option of creating a mixed forest. Species that are ideal for this purpose are Privet and Chinese Elders. These semi invasive species are ideal bonsai material as they are fast growing, have robust trunking characteristics with rich upper foliage leaf structure. Finally, don't dismiss the option of creating a bonsai forest using succulents. The Jade or Money Tree is fast growing and easy to root, producing an attractive tree using simple snip and grow, and loose wiring techniques. With a forest planting, when it comes to aesthetics, the layout and linear perspective are extremely important factors to consider. In the chapter 'Infinity & Beyond' I explain the illusion of perspective and the conventions related to number theory, both Japanese and Chinese. I will reference the principles of Renaissance Art and

discuss the concepts of focal point, negative space and their influence over the placement and number of trees in the pot.

The possibility of terminal transplant shock is always a reality and can be unsettling. For this reason I have committed a chapter to the causes and cures of 'transplant shock', ensuring your trees live longer and remain healthy. The need to undertake root pruning, repotting and branch or trunk restructuring in the correct season under the right conditions is vital to the survival of every bonsai. To help with that decision making, I have inserted a chart on page 17 to highlight the critical dates for each meteorological season. Summer heat can be a killer and on page 48, I show you how to build a simple humidity bath to minimize the dehydrating effect of the summer heat. Allowing you to have happy holidays without worrying unnecessarily about your neighbor forgetting to water your bonsai.

There are many books, blogs and videos on Bonsai, and it is not my intention to simply add yet another encyclopedic compilation on pruning and repotting. Bonsai is a way of life, so in this book I have focussed on examining the techniques that will refine your bonsai skills. The mesmerizing imagery of a bonsai forest doesn't happen overnight and so it is not surprising that the activity of designing and planting a bonsai forest will fully engage your mental processing. It is an orchestration of time reckoning over multi year cycles, ensuring your bonsai's are always work in progress. And it is this ongoing process of botanical rebalancing that intensifies the pleasure you get as your forest matures.

The genesis of a bonsai

If you don't already own a bonsai tree, the question that everyone has is.. "where do I begin". My suggestion is to adopt a three prong approach. To satisfy your immediate interest I recommend you buy at least one or two existing bonsai trees that are already planted in a traditional ceramic bonsai pot. This will quench your immediate need to own a tree and inspire you to keep going. Once you are comfortable with your day to day management of these trees, you need to advance to the next stage. The following two options will foster your interest and engage you more fully with building your future collection and planning your forest. Buying your first bonsai isn't as mind-bogglingly difficult as you think. The only obstacle that you may encounter is the array of sickly looking bonsai trees, which you will find in the mass merchandising displays at malls and garden centers. In many cases, these trees are not of good quality and are nothing more than immature nursery shrubs. These plants or saplings will be 2 years or less in age and would have had a slight upper foliage prune in the previous six month period. Invariably a small length of wire will be wrapped around one branch to promote the bonsai mystique and the tree placed in a standard ceramic bonsai pot with a poor draining soil. Basicaly the tree is being used to up-sell an over priced pot. To further mask any deception there may be a segment of moss or a thin veneer of crushed red lava rock covering the soil. Such displays are designed for impulse shoppers hunting out a present.

When it comes to buying a bonsai, you need to seek out a reputable professional bonsai retailer or devotee of the art. For your first bonsai, it helps if the seller is able to tell you the age of your tree and provide an outline plan as to when you need to repot or when to remove any wires. I would suggest your first tree should be a hardy and non deciduous specimen such as a conifer with a stylish looking trunk that shows evidence of where it has come from and how it may develop in future years. The lessons that you can learn from maintaining and developing an existing tree are numerous. These inspirational influences are necessary because your sapling developments may be at least two years in the growing before you are able to mimic the style of a bonsai.

The next option is a nursery shrub or small tree from a garden center. However this is not as simple as it might seem. You may need to visit more than one garden center, before you find an ideal specimen. Look for a shrub or small tree that has a good trunk and branch structure and will lend itself to providing design options going forward. Your first steps may involve reshaping the plant by radically reducing or pruning a number of branches. I will review pruning techniques in latter sections of the book. Be prepared to

A garden center shrub. Casual chaos or temporal paradise?

leave the plant in it's original pot for six months to a year . Repotting out of season, including further defoliation or root pruning at this time will inflict a fatal blow to any future hopes.

From saplings to trees

The final option is where I have devoted most of the content for this ebook. The process of developing your own saplings into bonsai trees, provides a high level of satisfaction for all budding (excuse the pun) bonsai devotees. Nurturing and styling a bonsai from a sapling is a medium to long term project. The results are not instantaneous as the transition to bonsai is gradual. This is where you learn to work in harmony with your plants and with the climatic conditions that make up your environment. You will experience some losses in the early years but as you develop in the subject and gain greater knowledge and an affinity for the limitations of each type of sapling, your losses will reduce. Not surprisingly, many of the best tree saplings for training into bonsai are actually invasive species, as this type of tree is more hardy and has a growing habit that helps the sapling to recover faster following it's initial uprooting and any subsequent pruning and repotting. In most cases these invasive species have attractive trunk structures that support early shaping and leaf trimming. You will obtain especially good results with Privet saplings and saplings that have developed from suckers on the runner roots of trees such as the Persian silk tree (Albizia julibrissin). I also consider most Conifer species as fitting the profile for being invasive trees. When selecting and scavenging these saplings, look for trunk configurations that have developed an interesting kink or angle. This may save you from having to shape, prune or wire at such an early stage in the development of the sapling. Not all the saplings foraged by you will be invasive tree species. The non invasive options grow at a much slower rate and consequently may be more sensitive to transplanting and pruning stress in the early years. One such

sapling is the Tea Camellia also known as Camellia Sinensis. The Camellia is an interesting and smallish evergreen shrub tree with semi fragrant white flowers and clean looking branches. Unfortunately you may find it's survival rate only averages 50% after two years, as the Tea Camellia doesn't like being stressed by repotting, leaf reduction or pruning in the initial stages. Apart from trees, there are other saplings that you can source from the ground soil beneath any number of interesting shrubs. However with shrubs you really need to allow the sapling to develop into a partial mirror image of the actual plant, to more effectively plan its future shape. The stakes can be high and it is for this reason you may find it easier to source tree saplings rather than shrubs.

Suitable selection

Trees

Judas Tree, Liquidambar, Holly, Ginko, Flowering cherry, Cypress, Cumquat, Lemon, Beech, Birch, Pomegranate, Hawthorn, Chinese Elms, Maples, Melia, Privet, Persian Silk, Larch, Cotoneaster, Cedar, Apricot trees, Cooper beech Sophora, Thuya conifers, Norway Spruce, Ficus Benjamina, Oak, Chinese Golden Larch, European Rowan, American Mountain Ash, Olive tree.

Shrub trees

Azalea, Variegated English Boxwood, Wisteria, Japonica (flowering quince), Ficus. Rhododendron, Myrtus, Nandina (sacred Bamboo), Ochna (Mickey Mouse bush), Crataegus (Hawthorn), Gardenia, Dwarf Pomegranate, Sananqua (Christmas Camellia), Tea Camellia, White Rata, Serissa (pink mystique), Lonicera (Japanese honeysuckle).

Succulents

Jade (money plant)
Adenium obesum,
Adenium arabicum
Crassula tetragonal (bonsai pine)

Constructing a bonsai forest

Plan your work and work your plan. This old axiom is one which I have applied for many years. The need for planning starts will in advance of planting your forest and involves prepping your saplings or trees prior to transplanting. There are any number of 'golden rules' with repotting and one such rule is that all upper foliage pruning, old wire removal and new wiring should be completed two to four weeks prior and maybe longer if your upper foliage pruning has been more severe. Then two days prior to planting out the forest, give your trees a thorough watering. Watering at this prior stage will assist the tree to over come any transplant shock. As it minimizes the pressure on the root system to maintain it's water uptake in the days following the re-positioning of your saplings/ trees. And on the actual day have your soils, tie-down wire, slab pot, willow water, muck and moss close at hand. During this phase you need to protect your plants from dehydration, so I highly recommend that you only remove each sapling/ tree, prior to placing it into position.

Pot, slab or slab-pot selection

Despite a slab or slab pot posing a more challenging environment for a bonsai forest, it has the benefit of projecting a more enhanced visual perspective. The flat and elongated surface of a slab or slab pot hints at true life forest imagery. Compare this with the alternative setting of a forest in a wide diameter oval or rectangular bonsai pot.

Positioning bonsai saplings and trees on an entirely flat slab may prove more taxing due to the potential for soil washout during heavy rain. If you shop around the various bonsai pot vendors on the internet, you will discover a hybrid design that combines the advantages of a standard deep based bonsai pot with those of a slab.

Pots of this design I refer to as slab pots and to demonstrate their aesthetics I have used some pots of that design in this ebook. The flat edges of these pots may still pose an issue with soil washout but this can be minimized by building a muck embankment. Detailed instructions and photos related to mixing and applying a muck emulsion are reviewed in the chapter 'Muck & Moss'.

Tie-down systems and drainage control

The standard method for securing trees in their pots involves either running a tie-down wire up through the drainage mesh on the base of the pot or if your slab or pot has pre-drilled holes for this purpose then through those locations. But if that is not the case, the next option is to secure the roots of your saplings/ trees to a lattice frame made from bamboo or wooden chop sticks (freely available from most sushi bars). The lattice frame is a simple construction that can be built with either wire or a glue-gun. The main advantage of using a lattice framework is the multiple potential tie-down anchor points across the pot. Once the tie-down wires are in position, you need only set about creating a healthy drainage layer over the bottom of the pot, using small stones and lava rock or pumice chips.

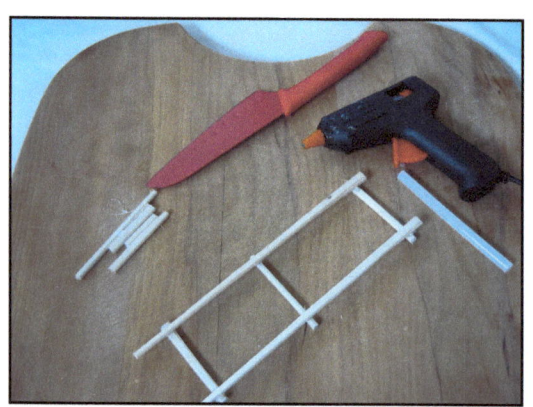

Foliage pruning

As tempting as it may be, the trees in an individual bonsai or bonsai forest should never be left to develop as an overcrowding 'mini me' version of the original tree/s. Unless you are planning to let the tree grow bigger, intervention is necessary to develop branch structure and for the shape to suggest both age and art. It is important to trim and prune often to promote the maturity and fullness of your tree. In my travels I have found a number of regional style variances when compared with the formulaic and idealized bonsai themes that underpin the common styles of formal and informal upright, slanting and cascade. This is especially obvious, in France, the Netherlands and Northern Italy, where foliage pruning is often limited to presenting a basic trimmed down dwarf version of the actual tree.   Whether it is with an individual or group forest planting, the 'trim only' pruning approach results in a bonsai that grows a dense canopy with excessive branching and leaf foliage massing in the crown as will as the central area of the trunk. If you choose to completely subscribe to the 'do nothing premise' you will miss the opportunity to add that element of awe. So don't be afraid to cut, pluck or wire. And when working on your tree or forest and formulating your ideas remember to occasionally step back and look at the big picture. If something doesn't look right then stop and do some 'foot dangling', before you rush back with the cutters. And try not to over prune a juniper as it take too long to recover, especially if you live in cooler climate zones. The quickest way to get to where you want to go is to take your time. Don't elongate time by being overly brutal with your tree.

The preferred season for undertaking any serious structural pruning is the autumn as it is a more pleasant and temperate season climatically and pruning at this time will allow you to rest the tree and forget about it over the winter. Then in the following spring when the sap starts accelerating through the xylem and the buds are looking like they are about to burst with new growth, you really are 'good to go' with any restyling you have planned as the next step in your project. This may be more bud pruning, a new pot, a root prune, some structural wiring or a general tidy up. But don't let me put you off the alternative pruning seasons of late winter and early spring. These periods are just as suitable for undertaking any structural realignment of branches and foliage, especially if you find a nursery plant which you instinctively feel may become an interesting bonsai. Remember that the outcomes you achieve today will form the basis for years of pleasure along with the admiration of your family, friends and neighbors.

Various pruning techniques

Pruning in preparation for a forest

The basic forest bonsai prune is very similar to the technique you might undertake annually on your fruit trees. Except with a bonsai forest, you are looking to add awe and build perspectives. Remember that you are shaping the style of your tree or forest by pruning and this can be as effective as using wire. The basic pruning formula follows:

- remove branches that are crossing and branches or stems that have turned back towards the trunk. Conflicting branches not only look untidy but may damage each other if caught in high winds.
- remove branches, stems and leaves that are growing within the inner perimeter of the tree and or growing downwards below the general plane of growth. Removing both downwards and inside growth allows you to appreciate the trunking of the trees and helps build better viewing perspectives.
- remove any trunk nodules, disjointed branch ends, and wild growth that looks unsightly.
- shorten branches to maintain shape and balance.
- if you need to limit upwards growth of the main trunk or branches, them trim the shoots at the apex.

Reducing the leaf size and promoting trunk forks

There is nothing worse that a bonsai that is allowed to develop an unimpeded canopy of oversized leaves, making it look out of proportion to the diminutive nature of it's pot and the general accepted norm of bonsai structure. The technique for tricking your tree into producing leaves of a reduced size is an integral detail of every ongoing monthly maintenance program. To reduce the size of most leaves and slow down the growth of your tree, you need only pinch back, trim or cut the existing buds and leaves on both your saplings and your bonsai. For non-deciduous (ever-green) bonsai, if you pinch and cut the leaves of your trees in late winter or early spring you will be rewarded with signs of new smaller leaves within 2 to 4 weeks. For deciduous bonsai the technique is slightly different and involves a method that is known as forced defoliation. Forced defoliation should only be undertaken in late spring or early summer on

trees that are in good health and have most of their structural framework complete. The method involves cutting with scissors every leaf at the point where the leaf meets the stem. Don't attempt to cut the stem from the branch in case you damage any dormant buds residing in that area. Within two weeks the stems will drop off by themselves and in the following week you will see new buds develop, marking the appearance of another generation of smaller leaves. But before you do anything, the first step is one of observation. The pattern by which leaves are attached to a branch or stem is a characteristic that will guide you in how you restyle the tree. This pattern structure forms the basis of your pruning plan in respect to which leaves and stems you should remove entirely vs those that you want to encourage. There are two main patterns of leaf growth, <u>alternate</u> and <u>opposite</u> and a less seen pattern known as whorled.

By definition:

Alternate leaves only have a single leaf attached at one node or location on a branch or stem. The leaves will then alternate from one side to the other long the length of the branch or form a spiral pattern along the length.

Opposite leaves refer to two leaves being attached at the same location on a branch except the leaves are positioned on the exact opposite side of the branch.

On occasions you may come across the whorled configuration. This is where two leaves originate from the same node or location, radiating outwards like the spokes on a wheel.

Your main goal has to be to re-style the shape of your sapling or bonsai by minimizing the size of their leaves. As discussed above, this is done by a combination of leaf cutting, pinching or leaf trimming i.e removing half the leaf because you do not want to remove all the leaves and reduce the tree's ability to undertake photosynthesis.

By selectively removing various alternating leaves or removing the alternating leaf of each opposing pair (going from side to side of each branch or sub branch) you will accelerate the growth of new and smaller leaves. With non deciduous trees, if your tree is healthy and strong, then you can also pinch away this new growth and force the bonsai into another cycle of new growth (new buds and leaves will form within 4 weeks). By maintaining this practice over subsequent years, the size and shape of the regrowth will become smaller with each new generation of leaves. It is normal practice to pinch away and limit any developing growth to only one side of the node. This produces an alternating pattern that will impart a more proportional style to

your tree. By selectively removing an opposing bud or leaf, you are mimicking the type of pattern that you see with trees that have the alternate leaf configuration. Throughout the summer season, keep pinching back new tips to trigger a more controlled development of new leaf stems and maintain the basic profile of the tree. If you are attempting to tidy up a tree that has been neglected or one that you have found in a garden center, the general rule is that you should cut off any growth past the third leaf. Then just wait until the new grown appears and either leaf pinch, trim or cut back completely to force further branches and leaf stems with smaller leaves. But don't root prune at the same time as the shock may well be too much for your plant.

The five plant hormones controlling size

The activity of pruning and defoliating sets off an interplay of plant phyto-hormones, that influence the development of smaller leaves and increased branching (ramification).

When maintaining and styling your bonsai, it is not a necessary to have a

deep appreciation of plant physiology concerning the ins and outs of leaf pinching or pruning. But if you have read this far, then it is likely you want to advance your understanding of the chemical interplay between the 'big five' plant hormones: auxin, cytokinin, gibberellin, abscisic acid, and ethylene gas(this is more a precursor rather than an actual hormone). There are a many variants for each hormone and there are other regulatory chemicals produced and stored in your bonsai tree. However the above hormones are the main factors regulating the effect that produces smaller leaves.

Auxin -controls tree elongation i.e. apical dominance

The apical bud on a bonsai tree synthesizes a family of hormones know as auxin. Auxins are mostly made in the tips of the shoots and roots, and will move through to parts of your tree where it regulates growth of the lateral buds. If the apical bud is removed, the source of auxin is lowered and then the lateral buds rather than the apical region will start growing. That is why you will observe increased ramification (branching) when you either 'trunk chop' or pinch out the bud at the top of your bonsai.

Cytokinins -promotes bushier growth

Cytokinins promote growth in the lateral buds. Plant growth and ramification is heavily influenced by the presence of cytokinins, working in conjunction with auxin or other hormones. For example, apical dominance is a balance between the auxin hormone which inhibits lateral buds and cytokinins that does the opposite and promotes cell growth and division. Cytokinins are strategically found in growth tissues such as the root zone where it will move up the tree to promote lateral bud growth. Cytokinin delays the aging process in leaf tissues by supporting the growth and duplication of the plant cells in shoots and roots prior to cell division (mitosis).

Gibberellins -controls stem and leaf elongation

They are a group of hormones that stimulate stem elongation between the nodes via cell division and cell elongation. Gibberellin is synthesized in the roots, the bud tips and in new leaves. This hormone acts in a manner that is a cross between auxin and cytokinin. How it functions is explained in the scenarios below.

Abscisic Acid - alerts the tree that it is water stressed

Abscisic acid is produced in the tips of drought'ed leaves and drought'ed roots. As a messenger, abscisic acid will move throughout the plant to inhibit cell division and alter the osmotic potential across the stomata guard cells, triggering them to close. This effectively protects the plant against excessive transpiration which minimizes evaporation from the leaves. Abscisic acid also works in conjunction with ethylene (see below) to abort leaves under dry stress conditions, further protecting the plant against evaporation. It also known to stimulate the growth of roots as this is the only way a plant can extent it's reach for new sources of water.

Ethylene Gas - produces smaller leaves and stunts growth

Ethylene gas causes a wide range of effects in plants. However in this instance as related to Bonsai, it works with the hormones above to slow down the growth of your tree and produce smaller leaves. Ethylene is produced when leaves are damaged by mechanical trauma such as leaf pinching and pruning or outright defoliation. Within the scenarios below I have detailed some of it's actions.

Scenarios highlighting the actions of the 'big five'

- ' Do nothing' to your bonsai.

Auxin levels are stable which creates increasing height. If you also leave the root area alone then the supply of cytokinin remains stable. As a result the ratio of auxin to cytokinin is maintained at a constant level which encourages normal upwards and outward growth.

- Styling and maintenance pruning of side branches and leaves.

The action of styling or maintaining your bonsai releases ethylene gas, and in the presence of auxin, you suppresses the side growth. Because you have removed a number of bud tips and new leaves, Gibberellin levels will be suppressed resulting in the development of shorter internodes. Consequently your bonsai will accelerate the development of greater height and increased diameter branches and trunking.

- Defoliation - aggressive pruning of bud tips and leaves and no root pruning.

The effect of defoliation causes back budding, shorter internodes and smaller leaves. With the apical growing tip removed, the synthesis of auxin is now limited, other than auxin being manufactured in the root zone. Consequently, with less auxin there is less elongation of the branches. However as cytokinin is still being synthesized in the root zone and auxin isn't present to block it's action, cellular division will accelerate in the form of 'back-budding'. And similar to scenario 2, the gibberellin levels are reduced thereby prompting shorter internodes.

Defoliate with care

Defoliation has a definite and measurable effect. Before you start, care should be taken as regards the health of your bonsai, the timing and the frequency of your defoliation. If you are in doubt, then I recommend semi defoliation over two phases. Defoliating results in back budding at the base of the axillary bud (petiole). By removing the leaf you will activate the bud to develop not just a new leaf but a new branch(ramification).

A deciduous tree should only be defoliated mid summer, after the spring leaves have fully developed. It is normally undertaken just once in summer unless you are brave and experienced enough to defoliate in early summer and then again late summer. But only if you live in a climatic zone that has extended summer and autumn growing seasons.

An evergreen tree should be defoliated in early spring after it has been repotted. Similar to above, if you are lucky to have long summers with mild autumns then you may defoliate again at the transition point between these two seasons. But don't push your tree beyond it's ability to regenerate as you don't need to be creating firewood.

Wiring

The objective for wiring any bonsai, is to both create and enhance a visually powerful branch structure, allowing for spaces between the growth layers of your tree and 'opening up' the outline of the trunk. If you are building a bonsai forest, wiring is also a tool that you can use to lessen any inter-branch conflict. You can only be guided by the tree, remembering that the shape and branch structure of your bonsai, will suggest any future line and style. There are occasions when the future style won't become apparent until you start pruning the tree and it is for this reason that pruning should precede wiring. I will not attempt to explain the technique of wiring as it is one of those tasks that is best learned by trying. It is not difficult, so long as you don't apply too much torsional bending to the branch and you protect it by clenching it with thumb and forefinger during the process of winding on the wire. Check Vimeo or U-tube for wiring demonstrations, then practice.

When to wire

The best time to wire a bonsai is when the trunk and branches still have some suppleness, as you are able to bend them without imposing too much stress. Normally, a bonsai is wired while dormant or semi dormant in the autumn, winter and early spring prior to or following a new growth phase. Junipers and conifers

and other evergreens will continue to grow throughout the year, although more slowly in winter, and can be wired during any season. Any new branches that have grown over spring or summer can be wired in late summer to position them, before they become more wooden and inflexible. Wire scaring is never desirable, however there are situations when you need to allow your wire to dig into the bark in order to permit time for the branch to hold it's new position. Any scaring will lessen and heal after two or three seasons. Care is required with soft tissue Japanese Maple trees as they develop rapidly during the spring & summer growth seasons, requiring removal of any wires after one or two months. In the above photo, the wiring was left in place far too long and the scarring is unlikely to disappear entirely. Depending upon

the softness or hardness of the branches and trunk, the wiring can be left in place for a period of six weeks to four months. Wire should be applied loosely on trees such as the maple and especially any succulent cacti that you might be training; such as in the adjacent photo.

However, conifers and junipers will take a lot longer for branches to set and it is not uncommon to maintain any significant trunk and branch wires for up to a year.

After six weeks or four months, whenever the wire starts cutting into the branch, remove it and if necessary re-apply the wire again if the branch does not hold. Wrap the wire around the branch in the opposite direction to minimize compression or scaring of the same plant tissue. Always use some type of bark protector or raffia if you need to apply more severe bending to

the main trunk or a significant branch.

If you split a branch, then stop bending immediately. Wrap it with tape or seal it with glue or pruning paste to protect the split. Also leave the wire on the broken branch to make it more secure. Do not attempt to bend that branch again for at least a year.

Ensure you anchor one end of your wire around another branch, the trunk or back through the drain hole in your pot. Also a useful technique that is worth practicing is to wire two branches using one wire. This not only makes you look skillful but provides an excellent anchor hold.

Selection of wire types

When it comes to wire, you really only have two choices.

There is the traditional annealed copper wire or the anodized aluminum wire. These days, the only time I use copper wire is when I am wiring up a Juniper. My wire of choice is anodized aluminum for all sapling and bonsai species. The problem I have with copper wire is that it is not only difficult to apply but once it hardens into position it becomes highly inflexible, requiring wire cutters to remove it. With soft tissue branches, it is very easy to damage your tree and break a branch when removing copper wire. But with the more woody branches on the Junipers you won't have this exact problem as you will require the strength and holding power of the copper to maintain your adjustment.

The strength of the copper wire does give you the advantage of using a smaller diameter wire compared to aluminum. So instead of a 5mm diameter wire, you may be able to get away with a 3.5mm diameter wire. Overall the size of wire that you use is dependent upon the size of the trunk or branch you intend to wire. So take care to not damage the bark with large gauge wire and for older more mature trees that require heavier wires, I would recommend you take the precaution of wrapping some synthetic water proof padding, tape or raffia fiber around the branch or trunk, before applying any torsional stress. The reason is that you need to protect the cambium from issues that occur due to cracking of the outer wood and any subsequent plant viral infections. With saplings, you should use the narrow 1.5mm diameter anodized aluminum wire.

Root Pruning & Planting a Forest

Root pruning & planting

To maintain control over the moisture levels in the root zone, it is essential you only work with one tree at any one time. It is because of issues related to moisture control and transplant shock, that root pruning and planting represents the most critical step when creating a bonsai or bonsai forest. When removing a pre-bonsai from it's transition pot, you will need to root prune before you place it into position. Even if you don't completely bare root the tree, you must clean most of the existing dirt from around the root ball. Once you expose the root system, rapidly identify what you need to trim and then reduce the main tap root. The dominance of the main tap root inhibits smaller horizontal roots from developing, therefore cutting is not an issue and will promote finer and more fibrous lateral roots over subsequent growing seasons. If you are constructing a bonsai forest and are using a slab pot, you will need to cut sufficient roots to ensure the tree fits it's new container, as it will lack depth. This may entail trimming back some strong secondary roots and any long fibrous small roots. During the process, don't allow your roots to dry out or expose them to direct heat from the sun. Once your tree has been positioned, spread out the remaining lateral roots, to help stabilize your tree and increase the contact surface area for root water capture.

If your your tree received a good watering (hopefully willow water) in the days prior to transplanting, then it will have an increased probability of a rapid recovery from root pruning. With the arrival of spring, the tree should not lapse into a state of transplant shock. The essential goal is to undertake pruning and re-planting in the shade and avoid the dehydrating effects caused by the spring sun. But remember not to 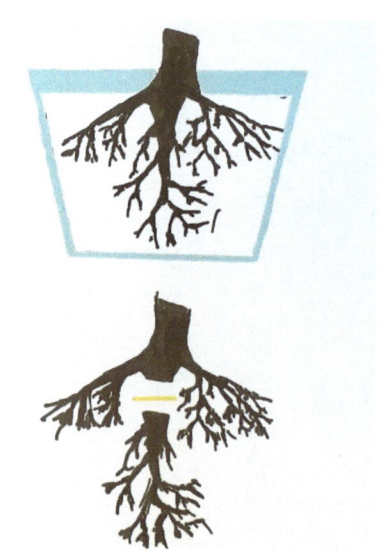 linger - if you prepared your tools, pots and soils before hand then you are better able to work at a relaxed speedy pace. Once the sapling/ tree is positioned, use a small trowel to build the level of the soil both underneath and around the root system. In the beginning only tie-down the roots loosely as you will need a degree or two of flexibility to tweak and semi re-orient your tree into it's final position. Depending on how close you plant your trees, you may need to trim or adjust the spread of the root system, to fit in with the roots of other trees within the forest. The final step involves securing the trunk and roots. Over a period of three or four years, the roots of all the trees will become interwoven and when it is time to re-pot the forest (note the extended period for a forest) you may need to repot the entire forest as one subject. The most practical solution is to remove the forest as though it is one plant and carefully prune the roots. Don't cut too much away. By reducing the spread of old fibrous roots along the outer areas and across the base, you will encourage new lateral roots and release some pockets of old soil. Old soil is one of the main reasons for poor bonsai health and disappointing results. But do not attempt to bare root your forest. Leave the old soil in the individual root balls and minimize any disruption to the intertwined root structure.

Finishing touches

Having planted and secured the bonsai forest, use a blunt tool (old chop stick) and probe deep into the soil to disperse any possible air pockets. This lessens the possibility of ants and other sap sucking insects discovering any hollow cavities for nesting or incubation.

Once you are satisfied with the distribution and elevation of the soil platform, you should apply a layer of muck to reinforce the soil embankment. This will limit any soil loss from water wash out. Finally add moss to cover the muck walls so that the forest has a more natural look. If you have a range of moss, plant more than one type as it builds upon the structure and color of the forest floor. But leave a minimum thirty percent of your surface soil exposed to air and light. For the next 4 weeks, leave your bonsai in an outside area that offers shelter and protection from direct sun, wind and rain.

The pressure is now off, and you can start to relax as you clean up the debris created during the planting session. After the event, it is quite common to discover a branch out of alignment or proportion to the tree and in the case of a forest grouping, a branch in conflict with other trees. Make a mental note and do nothing for at least two months. Give your trees time to adapt and develop their root structures, without imposing any additional transplant stress. It is important that these trees re-adjust fast and without any leaf trimming, branch pruning or wiring of the upper foliage will slow down the adaptation.

Meteorological seasons

● Northern Hemisphere

Winter	1 Dec - 28 February
Spring	1 March - 31 May
Summer	1 June - 31 August
Autumn	1 Sept - 30 November

● Southern Hemisphere

Winter	1 June - 31 August
Spring	1 Sept - 30 November
Summer	1 Dec - 28 February
Autumn	1 March - 31 May

Positioning in the pot

The mental process involved with both planning and planting a forest bonsai is similar to an artist conceptualizing the dimensional and visionary frame for a painting. The Renaissance artists who developed the technique of drawing in perspective, established a number of conventions that we now mimic when composing our own forest bonsai. Conventions such as the all important determination of focal point, the use of negative space, the interplay of proportion (big trees vs small trees) and how we overlap the alignment of our trees within the pot.

The objective of this chapter is to review the influences that can overwhelm us when it comes to the placement of the trees. Whether these factors are based on culture (lucky number theories), traditional bonsai shapes and styles or fantasy images in the form of rocks or cart tracks on the forest floor. If you want your forest to reflect the natural landscape, then you will need to understand some of the jargon and gobbledygook relating to the concepts of primary and secondary focal points, density, balance, and negative space. Over the following two pages it is likely that some of these aspects may seem intuitive. What ever the situation, it helps to read this material twice, in order to lock away these concepts in your creative mind.

At the point when you are planting your forest, you should have a general plan regarding the number of saplings/ trees, the overall dimensional requirements, the seasonal foliage colors and shape of leaves, and finally the type of pot required. Your first decision is to decide which sapling/ tree is the most pivotal and unique, as this will become your primary focal point. In most cases the primary focal point is not the largest tree but crucially it should never be the shortest tree. The unique shape and style of this sapling/ tree should be the reason you are making it your primary focal point. And as it is with art, the prime location for maximizing this perspective, is an off-centered position or the very front of the pot. A primary focal point that is located in the middle of your pot is not spellbinding to the eye. Having resolved this issue, the next most important aspect is constructing an area of negative space. Negative space is necessary in order to direct the viewers attention towards your secondary focal point and most notably for developing linear perspective while also acting as a resting spot for the eye of the observer. Negative space exists on two levels, the floor of the forest and the upper canopy level. Moss and interesting rocks on the surface soil are often added to provide greater emphasis, however an empty space may be just as effective. By design, a secondary focal point, might be a cluster of trees artfully arranged to overlap and advance the perception of a vanishing point. As in Renaissance art, a secondary focal point is either centered or clustered along one side of the frame. To establish depth you need only overlap the trees. This method enhances the visual appeal of your forest, providing views through the trees as opposed to the flat two dimensional aspect when trees are planted beside or behind each other in a contrived grid pattern. During this process, it is important to step back and visualizing the perspective of your forest from different angles, assessing which tree should overlay the view of the adjacent tree. At this point you may also want to consider creating hillocks, slopes or depressions in the soil. The significance of these varying perspectives will become more apparent a year or two after planting your forest. At which time you will notice the interplay of the trees and how sunlight filters through the foliage, creating patterns of light across the floor of your forest.

Infinity and beyond

For most people infinity is an inconceivable concept, yet somehow a forest bonsai has a potency that evokes an illusion of infinity. It was the ancient Greeks who conceived infinity as a boundless set of prime numbers. So if we were to create a forest bonsai based on a prime number of trees, i.e. 3, 5, 7, 11, 13..... then you enable that illusion, especially where the trees have a range of different sized trunks and heights.

Superstition or belief

Superstition is generally the enemy of enlightenment. However in the bonsai world it has a vast amount of significance, providing some guidance in situations where you decide to enhance the supernaturalness of your forest and project feelings of luck and fortune. Within the Chinese culture certain numbers such as 2, 6, 8 & 9 are considered lucky but the number 4 is very unlucky as it's pronunciation resembles the word for death. And in the Japanese culture, the numbers 4, 9 & 13 are unlucky. Both cultures agree that the number 8 is the most auspicious of all numbers. As a general rule, placing an odd number of trees in a forest composition provides an artistic and visually pleasing layout that looks less influenced by the 'hand of man'. So if you do decide on the lucky number 8, it is worthy to consider adding an asymmetrical effect by planting 3 trees on one side of your slab pot and 5 trees towards the other end.

When you next visit an art gallery, make a point to study the paintings of various landscape artists and note of how they conceptualized their three dimensional world using primary and secondary focal points, negative space, balance, color and proportioning of subjects. Your appreciation for general art and bonsai art will now be multiplied.

Techniques borrowed from the art world

Renaissance artists developed a technique to portray the three-dimensional world within the frame of a two-dimensional painting. The technique was known as linear perspective i.e. the idea that converging lines meet at a single vanishing point, with all shapes getting smaller in all directions with increasing distance from the eye. Later in the Renaissance period, artist expanded these techniques using colors and nuances of color (the use of red in the foreground and cool colors further back) and the use - or avoidance - of contrasts between overlapping forms. All adding or enhancing the concepts of negative space, perspective & focal point. To a lesser extent, these same conventions can be mimicked when composing a bonsai forest. This can be done using different types of moss, or planting different species of trees with varying color, heights and foliage characteristics. Also adding small rocks, using oblong pots, overlapping or misaligning the placement of trees -- all techniques that enhance the visual style of linear perspective.

Transplant Shock

Pre-bonsai and sapling transplant shock

Transplant shock is almost unavoidable, especially if you undertake a significant reduction in roots prior to repotting. Saplings sourced from the wild, undergo the greatest transplant shock, as it is easy to damage a large portion of their root system during removal. The survival of a sapling is a delicate balance between it's above ground and below ground needs. It is highly dependent on the health and functioning of the root system, so any disturbance in this area will inhibit the saplings ability to absorb water, nitrates and potassium from the soil. With existing (potted) pre-bonsai, the problem arises when you trim away excess roots, especially young lateral roots, during pruning and repotting. The symptoms of transplant shock become noticeable within a few days as evidenced by a sapling's general loss of vigor. If the transplant shock becomes protracted then reserve carbohydrates stored within the sapling, will be exhausted before it is able to recharge it's supply via photosynthesis. With saplings from deciduous trees, the leaves will normally change color, curl up and wilt unless steps are taken such as leaf reduction and further watering. Eventually all it's leaves may turn brown and fall off. However don't be too quick to throw your sapling out, as it may recover over subsequent months. With larger saplings, the shock might be less terminal with only limited dieback at the branch tips.

Conifers are different. Where there has been any trauma to the roots, the needles of a conifer sapling initially turn pale green before becoming becoming embrittled, turning brown and finally dropping off. Thankfully the negative effects of transplant shock may be lessened in a number of ways. The best advice that can be provided, is to limit any transplanting to the weeks between the last month in winter and the end of spring and again in the latter half of autumn prior to the onset of winter.

Transplant shock. One of those heart stopping experiences. Root pruned & re-potted in early spring then lapsing into transplant shock after 4 weeks. Eventually after 3 months (now early summer) new buds reappear but still have die back at the branch tip.

Proper watering is also an important post-transplant maintenance activity, but be careful to not over water your saplings or trees, as they will suffer as much from excess watering as they can from moisture deficiency. Use Willow water.

As a general rule, all transplanting or repotting should be limited to overcast days and undertaken in a sheltered corner of your nursery away from direct sunlight and persistent winds. To repot any tree or sapling during summer is risk taking, and may be terminal for the tree. If you are simply repotting an existing pre-bonsai, then it is recommended you give the tree a good watering the day before to ensure your tree is correctly hydrated. To reduce the impact of transplant shock, daily watering and keeping the upper foliage moist remains the most effective technique in caring for any sapling, pre-bonsai or bonsai. Use Willow water.

The transpiration debate

In the world of plant science there is ongoing debate as to whether the upper foliage should be reduced prior to or during the period when you transplant a tree. The hypothesis that supports pruning your tree contends that it lessens the transpiration needs of the foliage by balancing the reduced ability of any damaged or pruned roots to sustain the needs of your tree. However, opposing that argument, others will claim that pruning the excess leaf structure will reduce the carbohydrate storage and production capacity of your tree. There is no right or wrong answer. I recommend that when transplanting saplings, you do what you feel you need to do based on your own evaluation of the saplings condition and the degree of root damage that may have occurred earlier. However if you feel that you need to have a rule, then you can trim back the tree by limited leaf reduction and remove any unnecessary buds and small stems. It is also recommended that you wait at least four months before attempting any shaping or further foliage pruning. It is also worth pointing out that the use of fertilizer at this time is generally ineffective as the functioning of the root system is still impaired and may be unable to absorb nitrates and potassium from the soil until such time as they regenerates. For a pre-bonsai sapling that is already in a transition pot, you can follow the same guidelines except you will find that as the tree is more established, you will be able to shape and trim more heavily. But remember that any essential wiring should have been undertaken at least 4 weeks before repotting. And - before, during, and after this procedure, use Willow water.

After re-potting - wait patiently. Your sapling or bonsai needs a minimum of 4 to 8 weeks to recover from transplant shock. If the leaves on your tree begin to show signs of wilting or if it adopts a terminal appearance, don't panic. In more serious cases, depending upon the season, it is possible that your sapling or tree may take three months or more to recover from transplant shock. If necessary, water your tree with willow water for two weeks. Do not exceed two weeks otherwise you will promote increased root development and will need to prune early.

If there was to be a golden rule then it would be that no repotting should be undertaken out of season. It is for this reason that I have featured the seasonal dates for both the northern and southern hemisphere on page thirty two. Also as further precaution I would adopt a very critical eye with regard a number of Vimeo or U-tube videos on root pruning and wiring techniques. Not all but many, of these videos merge all the maintenance and styling techniques within the same time space. And even worst, these activities seem to be filmed over the summer season. This is both a brutal and terminal act for most trees and is likely the reason why you never see the same individuals recording a follow up video on the same tree.

Willow water

Willow water has been known for centuries but it's benefits mostly forgotten over time. It is a simple extract of two natural plant growth stimulants - Indolebutyric Acid and salicylic acid. Both these plant rooting hormones are extracted by soaking the branch or stem tips from any Willow tree of the genus Salix. So if you know where to find a weeping or pussy willow tree then you have access to the source material for the most powerful biological plant elixirs available. The general recipe for making willow water is to soak a large handful of thin willow stem-tips or twigs (reduced in length to 3 inches or 76mm) in 3 cups of water and leave to infuse for 48 hours.

The extraction process is enhanced if you start with boiling water. If you require a larger volume of willow water then scale up the quantities. There is no need to be overly exact in your measurements. The final yield of Indolebutyric Acid and the salicylic acid is more pure and superior to what you will get when you buy small containers of formulated Indolebutyric Acid in a blended gel or powered form. As a point of note Indolebutyric Acid, is a closely related chemical form of Auxin re. discussion on plant hormones (pg21). It is synthesized in the stem tips with the same basic responsibility for wound repair, stem elongation and root growth development.

Uses:

- Recovery from transplant shock - water your plant for one week using willow water if you think that your tree has gone into shock following repotting or root pruning.
- Air-layering - soak sphagnum moss in willow water before wrapping it around the branch that you intend to bud roots from.
- Saplings - water your saplings with willow water for the first two weeks.
- Cuttings - soak cuttings in the willow water over night before planting. continue to water the soil using willow water for the following two weeks.

Muck & Moss

Moss provides a compelling enhancement to showcase the style and imagery of a forest bonsai. Especially when moss is transplanted over the visual wasteland of a 'muck' reinforced embankment, built to support an elevated soil platform when using slab pots. Apart from the primary benefit of enhancing the imagery, moss is equally important in it's ability to retard the loss of soil moisture resultant from evaporation. The secondary benefit is that moss provides a quick indicator of moisture needs, evidenced by the moss taking on a dried and brown quality when watering is required.

Muck. Blending a batch of bonsai muck is possibly the most grungy of jobs that you ever do in relationship to bonsai cultivation. By it's nature bonsai muck is both sticky and dirty, and if your clay was soaking in water prior to it's use, then you'll be squirting yellow or brown water everything when you knead together the muck to produce a uniform and consistent mix.

Old gardening clothes are essential and if you want to keep the your finger nails clean then make sure you wear disposable plastic gloves.

With cleanliness in mind, it pays to have a bucket of water or a garden hose readily available for washing down your tools, your hands and any thing else you touch. Before you start, place all your essential items and tools within handy reach as you don't want to leave a muddy trail of clay stains. The essential items that you will need are: clay, coconut fiber, dark colored soil or black peat moss, scissors plus a spatula or old butter knife. The recipe for bonsai muck is simple. However before you get your hands covered in gluggy clay, first cut the coconut fiber to a length of 1 or 2 inches (approx. 2.5 to 5 cm). The amount you use is dependent upon the size of the job and the volume of clay available. However, as a suggestion, you should cut up at least one to two cups of uncompressed coconut fiber. If you can't find any coconut fiber then you can use pine needles, again making sure that these are not too long. The coconut fiber or pine needles help to add strength and structure to the muck reinforced barrier and also supports some water porosity. When making the muck, start by gradually molding the coconut fiber and dark colored soil into the clay.

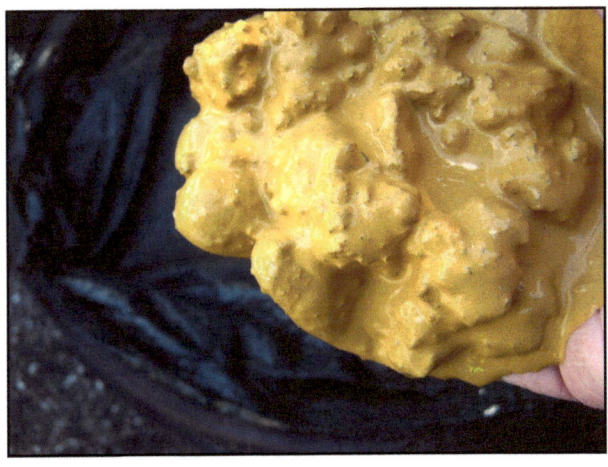

The clay needs to be kept wet and you need to be careful to not reduce the plasticity of the clay by mixing in too much fiber or soil. If it gets too dry and starts to lose it's sticky texture and plasticity then add more clay to the mix. This phase of the exercise is just like kneading pizza dough. Continue to mold everything to produce an evenly distributed mix. The more you knead the more elastic the final mix. If your clay has been sourced directly from the ground then it may sometimes have stones mixed in and you need to remove the big stones but can leave any little pebbles. If you find

your mix is too wet to pat into strips just place a good sized glob of 'muck' onto the embankment area then use a spatula or old butter knife to smooth it over the soil surface. Just like icing a cake. Neither making the coating too thin or too thick. Once the area requiring reinforcement is fully covered you now have a sticky substrate onto which you apply the fresh clean green moss from your moss garden. According to the Scientific American, there is over 10,000 species of moss, therefore it should never be too difficult to find a clump growing in a moist and shady area somewhere around your property. In recent years, moss has been portrayed as an invasive and troublesome weed by a growing number of household chemical marketing

companies intent upon selling hypochlorite based cleaning agents and water blasters. However, moss is far from ugly or troublesome and if you culture your own source of moss you will start to understand the fascinating and unusual nature of this plant.

Growing Moss is a simple enough exercise and it is well worth allocating a small amount of time to develop a few containers of weed and liverwort free moss. To get started you need to find yourself a source of nice looking moss. This could be moss that that has out-grown it's location within an existing bonsai container or maybe moss growing between the cobblestones on your drive or moss scavenged from underneath a tree in your local conservation reserve. You will find that the various species and genera of moss have their own specific requirement for light, water, humidity, soil and protection from the elements. Moss develops best under conditions of diffuse light. To reduce any moss die-back try to collect moss that grow in similar light and wind conditions to where you might place your bonsai. It is not unusual to find your moss goes through a form of transplant shock in the weeks following it's relocation.

A kokedama bonsai forest under construction. The saplings are Lacebark Elders (Chinese Elders). The saplings were established in a dense layer of silt and moss. The aesthetics of this will develop as the saplings mature. This planting is only a fun exercise and will remain work in progress for many years. A key element in the project is the rustic medieval appearance of the bonsai pot.

Transplanting moss involves a degree of trial and error, if not patience, as it may take at least eight weeks and longer before it gets established. As moss lacks the normal vascular form of roots found in other plants, it is vital to keep your moss moist if you want to maintain it's rich green color. There are some general guidelines related to how much moss you can add as a soil cover. Apart from the muck walled embankment, the amount of moss you apply should not cover more than 70% of the soil surface area for non conifer forests. But where you have a forest bonsai composed of Conifers (which are dry loving trees) you need to reduce the amount of moss to no more than 50% of the soil surface area. Conifers thrive best in dry conditions. As a note of precaution, do not allow moss to creep or grow up the trunk of any bonsai. As this softens the bark and leads to the eventual decay of the tree. Removing the moss using your best friend's toothbrush, is the simplest and least harmful method to scratch it away from the trunk.

Water - Drainage - Soil

Signs of overwatering

- Old and young leaves drop off at the same time
- There is standing water in your pot
- Leaves or needles developing brown patches with limited development of new bud growth and leaves
- A late and obvious sign of over watering is the growth of fungi or lichen on the soil

Signs of dehydration

- Stem and leaf wilt
- Leaves will start to drop off prematurely
- The edges of the leaves become brown and dried
- The lower leaves may curl and start to yellow

- Leaf, bud or needle development becomes very slow
- Leaves will develop a translucent appearance
- The soil pulls away from the inside of your bonsai pot or muck embankment.

Water

Transpiration never sleeps and is constantly demanding that the root system competes for water resources from the other trees in your bonsai forest. As we all know, the need for water correlates to the number of trees present, their size and the shape of your bonsai pot. Then there is the influence of your prevailing climate (sun, wind & rain) and the ambient temperature. All these factors combine to influence the amount of transpiration occurring within your forest bonsai and the ultimate level of moisture remaining within the soil of your pot. Your forest bonsai will definitely require more water during the hot, dry and possibly windy months corresponding to spring, summer and autumn. However, the winter rains may supply sufficient moisture to help your tree through the winter unless it is unseasonably dry. With the changing weather patterns you will need to maintain an awareness of the weather forecast and hold the thought that you might need to water your bonsai at least twice a week in winter. Especially if your forest is positioned in a sheltered area such as under eaves or is positioned on a veranda.

If you have left your forest outside in the 'snow' - as we do with conifer bonsai - be mindful of winter sun scald. (re the chapter: As Winter Descends)

If you have a forest bonsai growing in a slab pot, then water management becomes more critical. Early dehydration or a break down of the 'muck' walls may occur if your slab pot has been positioned in direct sun for most of the day. With a forest bonsai it is less likely that over watering poses the same problem as it does with individual trees. But when you have a slab pot or similarly shallow pot and an elevated soil platform, then water wash out may become an issue. The daily ritual of 'watering' is the ideal time to conduct a quick wellness check of your trees and a review of any maintenance or styling needs. These maintenance checks should also include checking the integrity of your muck embankment and the health of any moss growing on it. Attempting to grow moss on the muck wall may become an issue if there is limited water migration through the embankment. Where you have an elevated soil platform it may take a while to learn how the water disperses through the soil structure, so be patient and observe and replace any moss that starts to look dried out. Forest bonsai require water daily over late spring, summer and early autumn, however during the winter months you may be able to reduce your watering to twice a week. The key to proper watering is to allow the soil to dry out slightly between each application, as this allows the roots to extract the oxygen they require.

Drainage

Similar to the problem of over watering and under watering, bad drainage and any resultant growth problems arising, is caused by either excessive drainage or poor drainage. If there is excessive drainage from your pot then your forest bonsai will suffer from 'water stress' as you will now need to water more frequently and in small amounts to maintain moisture within the larger interwoven root zone of the forest. In cases of poor drainage, you will end up with soil compaction and a perpetually wet root system which is generally the cause of root disease, iron deficiency, and other growth issues that limit longevity. Do not let your soil dry out completely. I mentioned earlier that the key to proper watering is to allow the soil to briefly dry between each application. However depending on your soil mix you might find that if the soil dries out too much, it will develop a hard surface layer that won't effectively absorb water. And if the soil becomes too dry, then it may also start to retract from the sides of the pot or 'muck' embankment. So while you may think that you are watering your bonsai correctly, the water is actually flowing across the surface of the soil and down the inside edge of either your pot or muck embankment before channeling out

A continually wet root system will cause a conifer to turn yellow and develop areas of needle die back

through the bottom drain hole. This leaves your bonsai in a perpetual semi dry condition. This condition is most likely to happen over winter when your forest trees are under a shelter such as a veranda and you forget about watering as your trees are not in view. If this happens, I suggest that you immediately repot your bonsai, replenishing and repacking with fresh soil mix and also repack the muck embankment.

Soil type

A soil with high porosity will absorb water more quickly and drain more rapidly. Therefore if you have opted for a mix with too much lava rock, pumice or other inorganic material then you need to water your forest bonsai more frequently. Otherwise repot the forest using a potting mix that has less crushed rock or stones. Conversely, if your saplings or bonsai are in a soil mix of lesser porosity with a higher ratio of organic potting material, then the soil will absorb water more slowly as it retains a higher level of moisture. In this situation, you need to apply the water more slowly to avoid any compaction of the soil within the pot.

Root rot

Phytophthora cinnamomi or root rot is a common cause of plant demise for many botanical and horticultural plantings, including bonsai trees. The spread of Phytophthora or root rot is influenced by wet soil conditions. As it is the saturated wet nature of the soil that assists the movement of flagellated fungal spores towards the host root system. These spores subsequently penetrate the healthy roots and develop myclelium, which in it's worst case will form a white mass of branched filament hairs or hyphae. Once the fungus filaments take hold, the tree's ability to uptake water and minerals from the soil becomes limited and the tree quickly loses vigor and weakens. The first visual sign of root rot is seen in the foliage with one or all of the following conditions occurring: yellowing of the leaves, wilting and leaf drop or shoot tip die back.

If you suspect root rot, then isolate the tree and remove it from it's pot. Initially, root prune any diseased looking, black colored, roots then repot the tree in fresh free draining soil. Following the root prune, it is likely that your tree will suffer from transplant shock which may last for a period of three or four months. If it survives and you get regrowth then you have had a lucky save, but if the bonsai or sapling doesn't improve then it is time to consign your tree to the trash.

Happy Holidays

Line the base of the container (humidity bath) with river stones then cover the stones with crushed lava rock or river sand. Add water up to the level of the crushed lava rock.

The moisture will create a mild humid environment and diminish any fear of your trees drying out.

On return from your holiday, snip away at any random root growth that may have grown through the drainage hole of your pot.

Happy holidays are not happy if you forget to water your bonsai.

To protect your trees from drying out, use a plastic container to build a humidity bath.

Position your bonsai trees on the surface of the lava rock and place the container in a sheltered and shady spot.

If you are on holiday for longer than a week you will need to organize a friend or neighbor to monitor the water level and replenish up to and just below the surface level of the lava rock.

Insects and Biodiversity

Pantry based fungicide

For a low cost effective treatment

1 gallon (4 ltrs) water
1 tablespoon of baking soda
2 1/2 tablespoons of vegetable oil.

Mix together with a good shake or stir and spray on the affected bonsai. To maintain this emulsion you will need to shake the mixture periodically between applications.

Insects and biodiversity

Given a healthy & bio diverse garden setting, your forest bonsai should not have to suffer from too many pests or fungal infections. So when you combine a bio-diverse setting with the elements of wind, rain and sun, the population of bugs and fungal spores should be substantially lessened. But life is never that simple and you need to be aware that along with nature, there are times when you may also need to undertake some natural spray treatments to ensure that your forest trees are maintained in a disease and bug free condition.

If you live in a tropical or semi tropical area of the world, then your risks are definitely increased because bugs have multiple life cycles, as there is no winter frost or snow to kill them off. Bugs and fungal infections will likely migrate to your forest bonsai from infected trees and shrubs within your garden. So normal garden hygiene around your property during the autumn months is absolutely critical to limit the impact of adult pests that winter over within piles of leaf mulch. Over winter these pests are sitting out the season waiting to invade your bonsai collection once the warmer spring temperatures arrive. The moral of this story is that you need to sweep and dispose of all autumn leaves and piles of cut grass that you have been reserving for mulch. Otherwise relocate your bonsai and sapling collection. To combat any bug or fungal infection, there are plenty of simple tricks and inexpensive organic treatments based on natural pantry based formulations. These are highly effective against most pests, so long as you plan and act before too much damage is done. However, before you start treatment you need to try and identify the type of insects and type of damage that is occurring.

Chewing insects

These non stop eaters can damage all or just part of your plant. The more common ones are: caterpillars, beetles, grasshoppers, leaf cutter wasps and some bees. Chewing insect will leave your bonsai with either missing leaves or leaves with holes that start to discolor within days of being attacked.

Leaf piercing & sucking insects

I have a particular dislike of aphids followed by whiteflies and a range of other scale insects commonly known as leafhoppers. These insects need to be banished as they have one of the fastest reproductive cycles in the insect kingdom and will not only spread disease but become a potential infestation overnight. These insects are the ultimate sugar junkies of the insect kingdom and using their proboscis needle like beak they will suck the life out of your bonsai by mainlining into the nitrogen sap transport systems in the leaves on your tree. They are easy to spot once you learn to identify the various forms of damage going on with your bonsai. Look for mottled brown or yellow discoloration or dead spots on the leaves or a general overall wilted and curled appearance of some leaves and small petals. Sucking insects will unfortunately defecate a sticky liquid from the digested sap that is often referred to as honeydew. The honeydew builds up on the underside of the leaf and it is this residue that becomes the home for a dark grey fungi that is commonly known as sooty mold. Thankfully the fungus is simply a cosmetic matter as it does little harm to the bonsai, just merely blocking sunlight and sometimes causing a yellowing of the leaves.

Leaf rasping & sucking insects

The rasper - suckers are exactly that. Using their mouths, they will scrape away the outer cells from the surface of the leaves on your bonsai then suck up the sap ooze from the damaged area. The most common rasper - sucker is the spider mite. The surface of the affected leaves will turn brown and eventually take on a bleached and dry appearance. These little critters will also secrete honeydew that in turn acts as a host medium for sooty mold.

> Neem oil application dose rate
>
> A sprayable formulation is made by mixing 1 teaspoon of Neem oil in a quart of warm water (5 ml per litre) plus 1/4 of a teaspoon of dishwashing solution to assist with emulsification

Treatment can be simple

Initially I would recommend you isolate your bonsai from all other surrounding bonsai and garden shrubs then apply my two step treatment approach outlined on page sixty two. After applying the emulsion you should spray your forest bonsai with water, to wash off any residual detergent. If you find insects are still visible, you can either brush them off or squish them between your finger and thumb. If you are experiencing a rapid explosion in the growth of insects then use an organic pyrethrum spray, but you need to be mindful that there is a risk that this may also inhibit the beneficial insects (spiders, ladybugs, parasitic wasps...) which normally feast on a meal of aphids, leafhoppers and other mites. If you are keen to ramp up your attack with a broad spectrum and organically acceptable chemical then use Neem oil. Neem oil is fully biodegradable and provides an effective 'attack agent' against all the insects that want to chew, rasp and suck the sap out of your bonsai trees. Neem eliminates aphid, whitefly, mites, scale, and mealy bugs. It is also effective against sooty mold and other fungal diseases including black spot, rust, and powdery mildew. And as an organically acceptable product, Neem oil is non toxic to mammals, birds, earthworms and beneficial insects. Mealybug needs special mention. If it were not for it's white cotton like web you would not notice how quickly it can spread across the axial nodes of your bonsai. It is specifically evident in late summer and like all sucking insects it is a prolific breeder. The Mealybug is not susceptible to treatment by water based solutions, so you will need to use an oil based spray such as Neem Oil. Where you have Mealybug, remember to repeat your spray over subsequent days in order to knock out any newly hatched bugs. Unfortunately any natural predators such as ladybirds and parasitic wasps will fly away when you use Neem oil – so it comes back to the same old question – spray or not to spray.

Biodiversity

The key to biodiversity is establishing a garden of companion plants which over time will host a number of beneficial insects, who take nourishment by feeding on any chewers and raspers that are sucking the sap out of your bonsai trees.

To eliminate aphids, spider mites and leafhoppers you need to entice a vast range of their natural predators into your garden or onto your balcony. The good guys are - lacewings, hover-flies, ladybirds, silvereyes and parasitic wasps. All these guys enjoy a diet of aphids along with eating any number of other rasper suckers and their larvae.

There is nothing new about natural organically based remedies for inhibiting insect and fungal infections. It is widely written that prior to the 1800's, gardeners would even pull grass out of their lawns to make room for dandelions and other useful weeds or herbs such as chickweed, pennyroyal and chamomile. However I am not suggesting you do the same. As I take as much pride in my weed free lawn as I do with my collection of forest and standard bonsai. If you have a garden nursery and development area set aside for your saplings and bonsai trees (especially if your garden is a balcony apartment) then you can lessen your dependence on the spray bottle by growing the following plants within close proximity to your bonsai trees. They may be either grown in attractive terra cotta pots or planted directed into the soil. Many of these may also be used as cooking herbs or spices. But please consult the internet to verify that what you are about to ingest isn't toxic, such as cherry pie. As a suggestion the following may be grown in order to attract a range of useful parasitic wasps, bees, hover-flies and ladybugs, that will repel most of your aphids and mealybugs and other annoying pests or fungal blooms.

Cherry pie. Plant in a location near to your bonsai collection. It's fragrance will attract parasitic insects that feed on the rasping and sucking insects that damage your bonsai.

Cherry Pie - Either plant direct in the soil or into a large pot and position amongst your bonsai trees. It has a beautiful old fashion flower and leaf structure not forgetting it's remarkable and intoxicatingly rich vanilla smell.

Catmint - Not to be confused with Catnip which looks similar and is jokingly known as 'kitty cat marijuana'. Catmint like all variants belonging to the mint family of plants, has a wonderful spicy mint smell. It is a hardy plant with small lavender blue flowers in the spring. Regular pruning encourages more flowers and keeps it looking presentable in it's pot. And an aside thought... if you have a cat then plant some 'catnip' in a large diameter pot for your feline friend to sleep on.

Pennyroyal - Pennyroyal grows in amongst the grass on my lawn. It has a strong fragrance similar to spearmint and when the grass is mown it releases a most delightful mint fragrance. In addition to the above you can also grow: Spearmint, Fennel, Chamomile, Chervil, Chives, Garlic, Marigold, Yarrow.....

Companion planting and home formulated treatments based on garlic, baking soda, cooking oils and washing up detergents are not only easy but one of the cheapest and most pleasing of all methods to combat bugs and lessen your workload and anxiety.

Let nature become the guardian of your saplings and bonsai trees and when you need a more aggressive approach to combat the sap sucking feeding habits of various insects then use the pantry based remedies in this chapter or Neem Oil.

Two step treatment approach to combat aphids, spiders mites and other insects

Method 1

Using a hose - - spray the bugs off with a jet of water.

Method 2

Make up this simple emulsion:

2 tbsp (15 mls) dish washing liquid, 2 tbsp (15 mls) of cheap cooking oil and 3 cloves of garlic. Placed everything into a high speed blender along with a 1/4 of a gallon (1 litre) of water.

Leave your emulsion to stand for 12 hours before filtering out the solids. Pour the liquid into a spray bottle and squirt directly onto the mites and aphids. Repeated again after two days. Unless you have a total invasion taking place, try not to blanket bomb your bonsai to avoid harming any beneficial insects such as the ladybird or ants.

As Winter Descends

' It is the life of the crystal, the architect of the flake, the fire of the frost, the soul of the sunbeam. This crisp winter air is full of it.'

~ *John Burroughs (Winter Sunshine - essay -1875)*

Winter bites with it's teeth or lashes with it's tail. And when it is about to descend, we need to take a few precautions to protect our bonsai. Winter can be a difficult time for both normal bonsai and forest bonsai, especially now days with the unpredictable and out of sync weather patterns that we are experiencing across planet Earth. Events such as high velocity winds, rapid cool downs, shorter days, late frosts or droughts followed by extreme rainfall. They all add to our challenges. If you live in a midrange climate zone with few frosts, then you will not have as much to worry about compared with those living in eco zones where you experience limited sunshine hours and temperature drops below 22°F (-5° C). But no matter where you live one universal truth still rules - we all need to have a winter plan. Damage to a forest bonsai may occur from any number of low temperature related problems. At the approach of cold weather, it is timely to consider relocating your forest from the open and exposed area where you displayed your trees over summer and move them to a sheltered area that offers greater protection.

I believe that when temperatures remain above 22° F (-5°C), then bonsai should definitely stay outside. To 'winterize' your Bonsai it advisable to relocate your trees to a sheltered location so as to protect them against excessive rainfall, extreme frosts or long periods of snow. If you have bonsai forests, avoid moving them to a windy location, as it is likely they will suffer some conflicting branch damage and possible stability damage to the soil bed and muck walls, due to movement action. If the roots are interwoven then there will be a significant combined force exerted by the upper foliage down to the root zone. The roots may end up becoming displaced within the pot and as they move, they may chaff against the tie down wires, causing cracks and splits to occur in the root tissue. The resultant stress for the bonsai will resemble the symptoms of transplant shock. Then any extreme temperature fluctuations and cold weather extremes during the dormant period (or after) at the time of bud development in late winter and early spring, may have a devastating impact on your forest bonsai. If you have any architectural features around your home, such as arches, soffits' or cornices then your forest bonsai should be placed under this type of shelter, at the first indication of frost or extreme rain.

If you live in a location where you experience more extreme temperature variances where hoarfrosts, cover the ground with frozen ice crystals, then you should consider moving your bonsai into an even more sheltered location such as a garage or garden frame house. Before shifting your plants you must first let them 'winterize' in order to trigger the natural dormancy phase. If they are moved into a protective shelter you need to ensure there is sufficient light to allow the trees to still maintain a level of slow growth. If any of your bonsai start to look stressed during winter, then it may be due to insufficient light or lack of watering. If your shed or garage doesn't have a window then install some artificial lighting. Generally the use of fluorescent lights is recommended as they don't emit any heat and won't dry out the soil around your bonsai. You also need to plan for some form of air circulation, as this will inhibit the growth of any powdery fungi on the surface soil of your pots.

Watering over winter - watering during the dormant period is still necessary and your bonsai must never be allowed to dry out. The opposite - too much water - can occur where your bonsai is left exposed to long periods of rainfall or snow melt. So it is important that your soil mix is free-draining. Also reduce any surface moss and remove any heavy decorative rocks from the soil to lessen compaction during this period. The moss on the muck embankment can be left in place. A dry spell with windy and unusually warm daytime temperatures in winter and spring will desiccate a bonsai extremely fast. To survive these winter droughts your forest trees especially, will need water just the same as if it were a summer drought, except less of it. Don't over-water in winter and remember you only need to keep the soil moist.

The most common causes of winter tree damage are:

Rapid and Extreme temperature changes

If your forest bonsai isn't completely dormant (not fully winterized) it may become stressed by sudden frosts. If there has been a mild winter, your bonsai is likely to resume it's growth cycle earlier than normal by two to four weeks. Any sharp drop in temperatures, frosts, hail storms or heavy rain at this time will cause injury to any new growth.

Low temperature injury - 'Frost Crack'

If your trees were freshly wired in early spring or late autumn and are left exposed to a sudden freeze, then the tree is vulnerable to a condition known as frost crack. Bonsai trees will remain vulnerable for a period of four to six weeks following any wiring as the cambium layer of the trunk or branch is still repairing itself after having been bent into a new position.

Conifers. Winter burn Sun-scald

'Winter burn' is a problem that affects conifers if they are left in a frost trap or in a fully exposed location, close to ground level without proper watering. This occurs when the soil in your pot becomes semi-frozen or covered in snow at the same time as the upper foliage of your tree is luxuriating in mild midwinter sun. What then happens is the semi frozen roots are unable to supply sufficient moisture from the frozen soil. This causes the pine needles on the sunny side of the tree to burn and turn brown due to loss of moisture. So it is vital that you keep your trees watered during any winter dry spell and consider a straw mulch over your pots if you are planning to leave them fully exposed to snow or frosts. As wet soil will act as an insulator and provide protection for the roots.

Natures setting

A bonsai forest is about creating a work of art and a moment of awe, balanced by a sense of inner tranquility. To quote Walter Pall (a leading bonsai artist based in Austria) "A tree in a pot is a tree in a pot, it becomes a bonsai when it speaks to your soul."

Unlike an individual bonsai tree, your sources for inspiration are not just the small forests or clusters of trees that we come across in coastal zones or wilderness areas. Those images may have an influence but a bonsai forest is about capturing the spirit of nature and thereby structuring an inward journey for the mind. In fact, it becomes a personal attempt to create your own continuum within the boundaries of a slab pot. In the early stages of development, your bonsai forest may look overly contrived and too ordered to have an immediate impact on either yourself or the viewer. But as the forest develops over subsequent seasons, the trees will mature in their setting and start to project the illusion of a boundless forest of noble distinction. What I enjoy most from my bonsai forests, is the structural alignment of the main trunks and the interplay of the branches between neighboring trees. The combined effect, giving rise to angled lighting and shadows as the sun filters through the foliage onto the soil and moss beneath the trees. By just letting your eyes flicker over your forest and ignoring any visual reference points outside the slab pot, there is a micro experience of infinity. This effect can be hypnotizing and at times it is difficult to walk away without glancing back for a final look.

A bonsai forests is no answer to combatting the issues of deforestation. But in your own small way, you will embrace your eco awareness and develop a deeper connection with the natural surrounds. And during those peaceful Zen like moments, you will need to guard against the talons of expectation, urging you to break your connection with both the 'wood and the trees'. Be mindful that too much, too soon and out of season is a guaranteed technique for converting a bonsai forest into fire wood. Deliberate and delicate are the traits of a bonsai artist.

It is now time to convert your thoughts into action by assessing your stock of trees and to create your own urban bonsai forests.

As always, turn off the mobile phone and allow your bonsai's to capture your complete attention. This is your moment in time to experience restful activity. Resist distractions.

Mindfulness over matter.

How to diagnose a bonsai obsession

- You avoid going away on holiday trips because you don't trust anyone to water your trees.

- You buy unique ceramic pots through online auctions, despite having no trees to plant in them.

- You find yourself wiring and pruning your general garden plants.

- When you go for a walk, you spent more time looking at the ground for saplings or unusual patches of moss, than you do looking at the scenery.

- You can't walk past a willow tree without breaking off a handful of stem tips for brewing a solution of willow water.

- Your home to-do list has more entries prioritized for bonsai maintenance than home repairs.

- You find yourself reaching across your neighbors property to unearth a sapling, never considering that this is stealing.

- When you discover a patch of dark-colored clay that would be ideal as muck, you can't stop thinking about how you might remove a shovel load without anyone noticing the hole.

- Every time you go outdoors you visit your bonsai collection.

- In a paranoid anxiety over disease or weakening of the main trunk, you buy a toothbrush for cleaning any trunk moss. This lessens any further conflict with your spouse who's toothbrush you have previously been using.

- You find yourself waxing eloquent to anyone that will listen, that your bonsai reflects artistic renaissance perspectives.

Copyright & fine print

Forest Bonsai
ISBN 978-0-473-35202-8

Copyright © C.L.Hunter, 2017.

Craig Hunter asserts the right to be identified as the author of this work. All rights reserved under International & Pan-American Copyright conventions.

Much of this publication is based on my personal experience with growing and developing saplings and bonsai trees. Although I have made every reasonable attempt to achieve a high level of accuracy for the content of this book, I can not assume any responsibility for errors or omissions. The information in this book is distributed "as is" without warranty or acceptance of indirect, incidental or consequential damage or liability to any person, entity or bonsai tree. Which means that you should use this information as you see fit and at your own risk. Your saplings and trees along with your specific climatic and environmental situation may be different to the examples and photos in this book and therefore you should tweak your use of my information and recommendations accordingly. Where I have used a product name or a named feature within the book, then this remains the property of their respective owners and has only been used by me as a helpful reference or explanation. There is no implied endorsement if I have used any proprietary terms. Finally nothing in this book is intended to replace common sense or other professional advice, as it has been written solely to inform and entertain the reader.

www.ingramcontent.com/pod-product-compliance
Lightning Source LLC
Chambersburg PA
CBHW041945110426
42744CB00027B/14